HIGHLIGHTS OF A FORUM

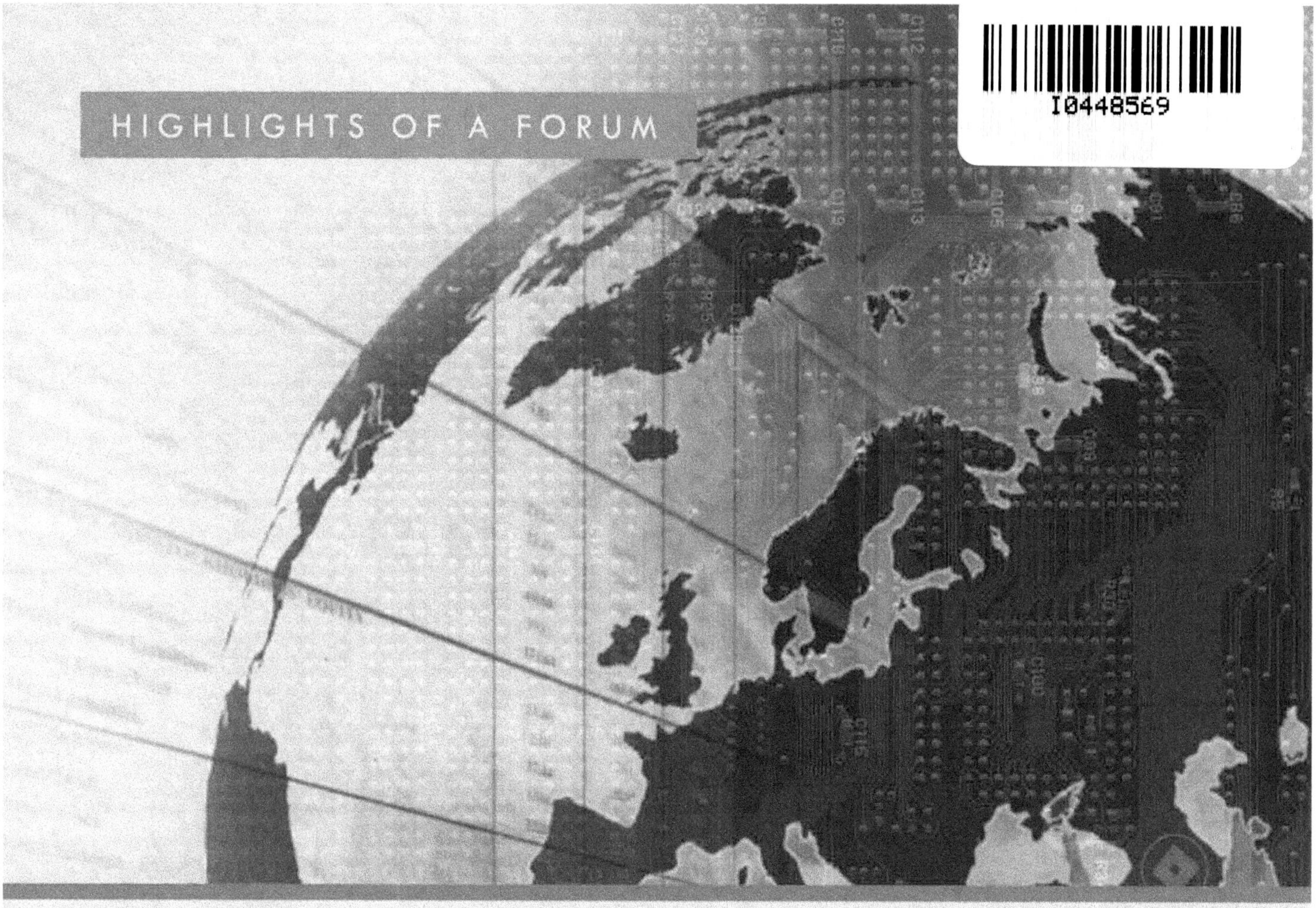

DATA ANALYTICS

FOR OVERSIGHT & LAW ENFORCEMENT

CONVENED BY THE

GOVERNMENT ACCOUNTABILITY OFFICE
COUNCIL OF THE INSPECTORS GENERAL ON INTEGRITY AND EFFICIENCY
RECOVERY ACCOUNTABILITY AND TRANSPARENCY BOARD

JULY 2013

GAO-13-680SP

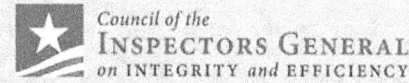

DATA ANALYTICS
FOR OVERSIGHT & LAW ENFORCEMENT

CONVENED BY THE

Government Accountability Office
Council of the Inspectors General on Integrity and Efficiency
Recovery Accountability and Transparency Board

Why This Forum Was Convened

Oversight and law enforcement agencies play an important role in eliminating fraud, waste, and abuse. Sharing data, knowledge, and analytic tools can assist government agencies in this effort. However, while there is a tremendous amount of information the government can use in preventing and detecting fraud, waste, and abuse, using and leveraging these data can be challenging.

In January 2013, GAO, the Council of the Inspectors General on Integrity and Efficiency, and the Recovery Accountability and Transparency Board convened a forum with the purpose of exploring ways in which oversight and law enforcement agencies use data analytics to assist in the prevention and detection of fraud, waste, and abuse, as well as identifying the most-significant challenges to realizing the potential of data analytics and actions that the government can take to address these challenges.

This report summarizes the key themes that emerged from the discussion in the forum. Specifically, the report discusses the challenges and opportunities in (1) accessing and using data and (2) sharing data. In addition, participants identified next steps to address these challenges and capitalize on opportunities.

Forum participants included representatives from federal, state, and local government agencies as well as the private sector.

View GAO-13-680SP. For more information, contact Steve M. Lord at (202) 512-4379 or lords@gao.gov.

What Participants Said
Participants identified a range of challenges and opportunities associated with data analytics—which involve a variety of techniques to analyze and interpret data to facilitate decision making—as discussed below.

Challenges and opportunities in accessing and using available data
Challenges participants cited include, among other issues, oversight and law enforcement entities not always being aware of all the data that may be available to assist them in their duties, and a lack of incentives for program offices to develop information-technology systems to support data analysis by oversight and law enforcement entities. Participants also noted other issues related to managing and using data such as challenges in developing a strategy to prioritize limited resources and the difficulty oversight entities face in measuring the success of fraud-prevention efforts.

Participants also identified opportunities to enhance data-analytics efforts, such as consolidating data and analytics operations in one location to increase efficiencies by enabling the pooling of resources as well as accessing and sharing of the data. Participants further identified strategies to garner organizational support for data-analytics programs, such as short-turnaround projects that produce quick, valuable successes to highlight the value of data analytics.

Challenges and opportunities in sharing data
Challenges participants cited include, among other issues, certain statutory requirements that place procedural hurdles on agencies wishing to perform data matching to detect fraud, waste, and abuse, and technical obstacles—such as the lack of uniform data standards across agencies—which make it more difficult for oversight and law enforcement entities to share available data. Participants also noted challenges in sharing data across federal, state, and local government agencies due to a variety of factors including actual and perceived legislative barriers.

Participants also discussed opportunities that could be realized if the government utilized and shared interoperable, open-source analytical tools and techniques, which could lessen the challenge of developing licensing agreements for proprietary software tools, be utilized at a low cost, and be tailored to meet the needs of individual agencies.

Next steps
Participants identified several next steps that the three sponsoring organizations agreed to implement, including: compiling a consolidated directory of data sources to increase awareness; compiling a library of available open-source data analytics, modules, and tools; developing an ongoing community of practice focused on data-sharing challenges; and examining the existing statutory framework to determine whether changes related to challenges and barriers for data analytics would be useful to oversight and law enforcement agencies in carrying out their missions.

GAO — U.S. GOVERNMENT ACCOUNTABILITY OFFICE

Council of the
INSPECTORS GENERAL
on INTEGRITY and EFFICIENCY

Contents

Letter		1
	Foreword from the Forum Hosts	1
	Participants Identified Challenges Related to Accessing and Using Data to Identify Fraud, Waste, and Abuse and Discussed Opportunities to Enhance Analytics Efforts	3
	Forum Participants Identified Several Challenges and Opportunities Related to Data Sharing across Government	10
	Forum Participants Identified Next Steps in Addressing Challenges	17
Appendix I	Forum Agenda	20
Appendix II	Forum Participants	21
Appendix III	Related Products and Image Sources	24
Appendix IV	Contacts and Staff Acknowledgments	27

Abbreviations

CIGIE	Council of the Inspectors General on Integrity and Efficiency
CMS	Centers for Medicare & Medicaid Services
Computer Matching Act	Computer Matching and Privacy Protection Act
DMF	Death Master File
FISMA	Federal Information Security Management Act of 2002
FOIA	Freedom of Information Act
FPS	Fraud Prevention System
HIPAA	Health Insurance Portability and Accountability Act
HIV	human immunodeficiency virus
IG	Inspector General
IT	information technology
Recovery Board	Recovery Accountability and Transparency Board
ROC	Recovery Operations Center

Foreword from the Forum Hosts

Recent financial and economic conditions have prompted greater scrutiny of government spending, highlighting the important role oversight and law enforcement agencies play in identifying and eliminating fraud, waste, and abuse. A number of government oversight and law enforcement agencies are using data analytics—which involve a variety of techniques to analyze and interpret data—to help identify and reduce fraud, waste, and abuse. For example, predictive analytic technologies can identify fraud and errors before payments are made, while others, such as data-mining and data-matching techniques, can identify fraud or improper payments that have already been awarded, thus assisting agencies in recovering these dollars. However, despite these efforts, the path to capitalizing on the potential of data analytics is not a clear one. While there is a tremendous amount of information that the government can use, identifying what data are available and then finding ways to analyze and use the data effectively are critical steps to moving forward.

In January 2013, our organizations convened a forum to explore these issues. The forum offered a series of facilitated discussion sessions (see app. I for the agenda). During the first session, participants discussed data sources that are useful for preventing and detecting fraud. During the second session, they discussed opportunities and challenges related to accessing and sharing data. The group then heard from private-sector participants about data-analytics tools—including open-source tools—that are available to assist in fraud prevention and detection. The group also discussed examples of how data are being used for oversight, and the challenges related to managing resources and prioritizing work. Participants completed the day with a session discussing how oversight and law enforcement agencies might address the challenges identified throughout the forum, and identified several next steps that our organizations agreed to implement. This report summarizes key themes that emerged during the forum. Specifically, the report discusses the challenges and opportunities in (1) accessing and using data and (2) sharing data. In addition, it describes the next steps to address these challenges and capitalize on opportunities.

Forum participants were selected to reflect a range of viewpoints and included representatives from federal, state, and local government agencies as well as the private sector. The forum was structured so that participants could comment on issues openly, although not all participants commented on all topics. This report—jointly developed by our organizations—summarizes the ideas and themes that emerged at the forum and the collective discussion of participants at the sessions. The summary does not necessarily represent the views of any individual participant or the organizations that these participants represent, including GAO, the Council of the Inspectors General on Integrity and Efficiency, and the Recovery Accountability and Transparency Board.

We would like to thank all the participants of this forum for taking the time to share their knowledge and insights on improving data analytics for detecting and preventing fraud, waste, and abuse. We look forward to working with them and others moving forward on the issues identified.

Gene L. Dodaro
Comptroller General
of the United States

Phyllis K. Fong
Inspector General
U.S. Department of Agriculture
Chairperson
Council of the Inspectors General on Integrity and Efficiency

Kathleen S. Tighe
Inspector General
U.S. Department of Education
Chair
Recovery Accountability and Transparency Board

July 15, 2013

Participants Identified Challenges Related to Accessing and Using Data to Identify Fraud, Waste, and Abuse and Discussed Opportunities to Enhance Analytics Efforts

Participants Identified Several Challenges Related to Accessing and Using Data

Oversight Entities Were Not Always Aware of the Data Available to Identify Fraud, Waste, and Abuse

Despite the vast amount of data available, participants stated that oversight and law enforcement entities were not always aware of all the data that may be available to assist them in their duties, which limits the abilities of oversight and law enforcement entities to leverage such data to better carry out their work. Prior to the forum, GAO, the Council of the Inspectors General on Integrity and Efficiency (CIGIE), and the Recovery Accountability and Transparency Board (Recovery Board) worked together to ask federal oversight and law enforcement entities to submit basic information on data sources they use in their efforts to identify fraud, waste, and abuse. GAO aggregated the responses and shared a list with participants during the forum. Participants agreed that the list was useful in helping them to gain additional awareness of available data, and suggested that additional information sharing about the data sources could further enhance their abilities to effectively carry out their missions.

Participants also cited an interest in finding ways to identify sources of information on known offenders, or "bad actors," that agencies identified as having taken advantage of the government in an abusive or fraudulent manner.[1] Participants generally agreed that the federal government could do more to share information about known offenders, and participants from both the government and the private sector recommended that efforts be made to increase awareness and share information on these individuals to advance oversight and law enforcement efforts. Participants noted that there is a wide array of data that exist about such individuals, such as individual Inspector General (IG) databases, public court records, and data on contractors and grant recipients; however, the information is not always collected or shared in a systematic way.

Program Offices Lack Incentives to Design Information-Technology Systems to Facilitate the Identification of Fraud, Waste, and Abuse

Participants said that their government program offices lack incentives to develop information-technology (IT) systems that would be useful for oversight efforts. Participants reported that, because of the lack of incentives, there is a general reluctance to develop systems that would be useful in identifying fraud, waste, and abuse.

Participants noted that while all agencies are concerned about fraud, waste, and abuse, the core mission of any program office is to administer the programs. As a consequence, participants stated that program offices generally do not design IT systems with oversight in mind. For example, participants explained that program offices responsible for providing benefits to members of the public are often focused on doing so as efficiently as possible and design their IT systems to assist in meeting this goal. In contrast, oversight entities focus on reviewing whether policies are being enforced regarding beneficiary eligibility and identifying areas where programs may be vulnerable to fraud, waste, or abuse, according to forum participants. Participants stated that because of the difference in missions, oversight entities may use program-office data in a way that is different from how it was originally intended, which can create challenges. Forum participants noted that oversight entities could better incentivize program offices to design systems conducive to oversight. In particular, one participant noted that oversight entities may have better success in persuading program offices to design systems with capabilities that go beyond their primary program mission if they can demonstrate how the added capabilities will be beneficial.

---

[1]For example, the Office of the Inspector General of the U.S. Department of Health and Human Services maintains a List of Excluded Individuals and Entities. Entries on this list are excluded from participation in all federal health care programs because they have been convicted of offenses such as patient abuse, health care–related financial misconduct, and other reasons.

Challenges Exist in Managing and Using Data and Measuring the Results of Fraud-Prevention Efforts

Forum participants identified several challenges related to managing and using data in their organizations and measuring the success of their efforts, as discussed below.

- *The amount of data available can often be overwhelming for oversight and law enforcement agencies, and developing a strategy to prioritize limited resources is difficult.* One participant stated that his office is overwhelmed with the number of investigative leads generated from its data-analytics activities. Participants cited various methods to prioritize work. For example, one participant stated that his office uses analytical methods to prioritize cases on the basis of the potential for a large recovery. Another participant stated that the fraud- prevention system her office uses incorporates a continuous feedback loop that refines the way the office prioritizes cases. In addition, senior management takes into account the amount of time that it will take to investigate and resolve cases when deciding where to allocate resources.

- *Participants cited various legal implications of owning and maintaining data.* Many participants said that efficiently allocating resources—and minimizing legal implications of owning and maintaining data—is key, and stressed the importance of a planned approach to acquiring the data. Agencies must consider many legal issues—including Freedom of Information Act disclosure requirements,[2] Federal Information Security Management Act of 2002 (FISMA) information-security requirements,[3] and protocols for records retention when obtaining data. One participant noted that once a government agency obtains data—even if they are acquired from another entity—the receiving agency may have a legal requirement to properly safeguard them and to follow applicable record-retention requirements. This participant recommended partnering with legal experts early on when acquiring data to better understand the different legal constructs and any limitations in how the data can be used. Participants encouraged a selective approach to acquiring data, noting that—given resource constraints—it is important not to try to gain access to all data, but to have a targeted approach in meeting specific objectives.

---

[2] 5 U.S.C. § 552.

[3] 44 U.S.C. §§ 3541-3549.

- *Measuring the success of analytics programs—especially in efforts to prevent fraud, waste, and abuse—is difficult.* Some participants explained that it is difficult to measure the effect of prevention efforts, that is, savings associated with funds that were never stolen or wasted as a result of successful data-analytics and fraud-prevention efforts. Some participants said that their offices are seeking to measure the success of their analytics programs by analyzing trends over time. For example, one participant stated that his office used to measure results by how much money was recovered and how many suspects were caught, but now, to measure prevention, the office looks at whether there has been a reduction in a particular type of fraudulent activity.

Participants Identified Opportunities to Enhance Data-Analytics Efforts

Opportunities Exist to Help Develop and Enhance Data-Analytics Capabilities

Participants highlighted several opportunities to apply lessons learned to develop and enhance existing data-analytics capabilities.

- *Knowledgeable and skilled staff are essential.* Forum participants stressed that having data and analytics tools are not enough; rather, it is crucial to also have talented staff onboard to perform data analysis and identify high-quality investigative leads and areas that are the greatest risk to the government. Knowledgeable and skilled analysts have the ability to see information well, understand how to go deeper into the data, and find complementary data through other sources. Participants commented that computers are no substitute for humans and there is no "find fraud" button; a computer can identify indicators but cannot perform the same kind of evaluation that a human can. For example, analysts can look at the results of a computer analysis and determine whether the pattern can be explained away or if there are signs of fraudulent activity. Another participant emphasized the persistent challenge in finding the optimal balance between people and computers.

- *Consolidating data and analytics operations into one location can enhance return on investment.* Forum participants said that consolidating disparate databases can help increase efficiencies by enabling the pooling of resources as well as accessing and sharing of the data. For example:

- One participant said that instead of many groups doing small-scale analytics in a limited way, creating one larger group could offer greater synergies and access to more resources. For example, a larger group would have enough resources to purchase data tools and systems that would have been out of reach for smaller groups.

- Another participant stated that sharing databases could create challenges without some level of centralization, where there is a responsible party for retaining and maintaining the database. Another participant explained that identifying an agency to serve as the custodian of those data would help ensure proper safeguards are in place to protect privacy.

- *Using predictive analytics to identify fraudulent claims before they are paid can be preferable.* Participants believed that benefits can be gained from moving from a "pay-and-chase" model—where agencies attempt to recover fraudulent claims that have been paid—to using predictive analytics to identify fraudulent claims before they are paid. Participants noted that recovering money lost due to fraud was difficult, and underscored the need to amplify preventative efforts. Some participants cited the Centers for Medicare & Medicaid Services' (CMS) Fraud Prevention System (FPS) as an example of a data-analytics system designed to detect and prevent fraud. This system—developed as a result of a statutory mandate—uses a combination of analytic models simultaneously to analyze billions of claims data to identify questionable claims for further analysis and investigation, one participant stated. Specifically, claims deemed suspect are referred for further program or law enforcement review, or both, and determinations are then fed back into the system. The participant said that this feedback loop is designed to allow for constant learning and for the predictive model to be continuously refined to detect fraudulent claims. One participant said that having a comprehensive team of experts is a crucial component of the program. For example, FPS teams are made up of analysts, statisticians, attorneys, medical professionals, and law enforcement personnel who meet together to solve problems collaboratively.

The Recovery Board's participants stated that the positive impact of the Recovery Operations Center (ROC) is directly attributable to the implementation of the types of opportunities and lessons learned that participants highlighted, such as consolidating government data in one location supported by state-of-the-art analytic tools and experienced highly-skilled staff who can leverage tools for data analysis. Recovery board participants noted that the ROC is uniquely positioned to serve the law enforcement community with this type of analytical support.

Garnering Organizational Support in Using Data Analytics Is Key to Success

One of the themes that emerged during the forum was the importance of building support within an organization for using data analytics to identify fraud, waste, and abuse. Participants discussed various strategies for starting a data-analytics operation and identified the following factors as being key to successfully obtaining institutional support:

- *Obtaining cultural acceptance across the entire oversight or law enforcement entity or both is important when building a data-analytics team.*

  - One participant shared his experience in setting up a data-analytics operation, stating that, in some ways, getting the data-analytics technology in place is the easy part; getting the technology accepted into the organization's culture was more challenging. According to this participant, to help ensure that the data-analytics technology is accepted into the culture, relationships across the organization need to be strengthened. Gaining cultural acceptance can be a challenge because it can be difficult to convince those who do not normally work with data to integrate data analytics into their work, another participant noted.

  - Another participant who has experience setting up a data-analytics system stressed the importance of having senior-management involvement and support.

- *Demonstrating "early victories" and a quick return on investment can help highlight the value of data analytics.*

  - One participant found that although calculating return on investment can be challenging, it is still important for agencies to demonstrate the effect of their work when asking for funding and other resources.

  - Another participant said that targeting short-turnaround projects that produce quick, valuable successes helped demonstrate the value of the data-analytics group and garnered greater support for subsequent efforts. The participant's office found that delivering early, impactful victories and results helped change an agency's culture to embrace data analytics.

- Another participant stated that part of the return on investment in data analytics is becoming a proactive organization in which investigators seek out fraud, waste, and abuse, rather than continuing to be a reactive organization that waits for requests from the outside.

- *Tailoring information to the needs of the end users so that appropriate action can be taken is important.* Several participants emphasized the importance of data visualization in showing the value of their work. For example:

  - One participant found that in reporting the results of the data analytics to stakeholders, there needs to be a balance between substantive content and presentation; communicating strategies or plans through colorful graphics had been far more effective than through an inundation of spreadsheets.

  - This participant found that combining high-quality data output with illustrative visuals has helped his data-analytics team gain acceptance.

  - Another participant shared that she worked with end users to find out what information they need for their investigations. In response, instead of providing investigators raw data and risk scores, she provided tailored information that investigators need in order to do their work.

- *Thoroughly vetting investigative leads generated through data analysis—to identify and remove false positives—can build credibility for analytics programs.* One participant noted that, from his experience, if his office had referred cases for investigation and they turned out to be false positives—namely, improper identification of individuals or entities that were not engaged in fraud—future referrals would be ignored. He stressed the importance of developing a process to vet cases before making an investigative referral. He noted that one of his team's recent analytical models identified 85,000 individuals associated with potential fraudulent activities. However, sending such a large output to the investigators for follow-up activities would have resulted in numerous false positives and an eventual erosion of faith in the work of his team. He therefore created a team to evaluate the results to reduce the number of false positives by comparing the output from the data analytics to other data sources before referring cases to investigators.

Forum Participants Identified Several Challenges and Opportunities Related to Data Sharing across Government

Participants Identified Several Challenges Related to Data Sharing

Legal Constraints May Hinder Agencies' Ability to Detect Fraud, Waste, and Abuse

Participants generally acknowledged the importance of the protections that privacy laws set forth; however, participants from the IG community and the Recovery Board noted concerns with computer matching requirements in the Privacy Act that they said were overly burdensome and hindered their ability to detect fraud, waste, and abuse.[4] These participants stated that there must be a balance between safeguarding privacy and increasing the transparency of data. The Privacy Act is the principal law aimed at protecting personal privacy, with an underlying purpose to provide certain safeguards to individuals against invasion of privacy with respect to the collection and disclosure of personal information and to provide citizens with certain rights and a degree of fairness regarding the use of such information by the federal government. In doing so, the laws require federal agencies to establish rules and procedures for maintaining and protecting personal data in agency record systems. The Privacy Act has been amended over time to require agencies to demonstrate the purpose and benefits of proposed computer matching programs and ensure due process and accountability.

---

[4]The Computer Matching and Privacy Protection Act (Computer Matching Act) was passed by Congress in 1988 as an amendment to the Privacy Act of 1974 (5 U.S.C. § 552a) to provide safeguards regarding an agency's use of certain records when performing certain computer matching programs. The Privacy Act of 1974 is the primary act that regulates the federal government's use of personal information. The Privacy Act places limitations on agencies' collection, disclosure, and use of personal information in systems of records.

- *Participants from the IG community and the Recovery Board raised concerns that the Computer Matching Act created impediments to government data collection and analytics activities to detect improper payments and fraud.* Participants from the IG community and Recovery Board pointed to the multiple steps and processes required by the Computer Matching Act, which often take a long time before oversight entities can use agency data for matching purposes. For instance, these participants said that agencies have slow processes for evaluating potential data-sharing agreements and that there is no incentive for an agency to move more quickly in evaluating and approving these agreements. One forum participant stated that a recent computer matching agreement took approximately 2 years to get finalized. Some participants noted that the Computer Matching Act generally only applies to a Federal agency's computerized comparison of its lawfully collected data against data collected by another agency to identify program eligibility or regulatory compliance issues or to recover payments or delinquent debts. These participants believed it significant that the act does not govern the agency's ability to acquire this data and—since it only applies to electronic matching—does not restrict, for example, a side-by-side comparison of two hardcopy lists of private information.

  One forum participant expressed his belief that adoption by agencies of overly conservative interpretations of matching requirements may be the true barrier, and not the law itself. This participant suggested that conservative interpretations could be addressed by demonstrating to agencies the value of sharing data and providing them with incentives to identify ways to work within current law to do so. Other participants agreed that conservative or incorrect interpretations of existing legislation represent a barrier and that opportunities exist to address this issue by reaching agreement on a common understanding of the law.

- *Some participants stated that certain provisions of the Computer Matching Act threaten IG independence.* Under the Inspector General Act, IG offices are established as independent offices within their host agency, and participants from the IG community raised concerns that provisions of the Computer Matching Act threaten the principle of independence.[5] They explained that the act requires, among other

---

[5]Inspector General Act of 1978, Pub. L. No. 95-452, §§ 2, 3 (Oct. 12, 1978). 5 U.S.C. App. 3.

things, that IG offices obtain the approval of the agency's Data Integrity Board in order to implement a computer matching agreement.[6] Although the act includes each IG as a member of his or her host agency's board, the majority of the board members are not officials from the IG office. Participants from the IG community expressed concerns that requiring these agency officials to approve an IG office–proposed data match could allow a board to prevent the match, or to impose undue restrictions or conditions on the match, thereby compromising the IG's independent ability to determine the scope and methodology of the IG office's audit or investigation. In addition, requiring approval from the Data Integrity Board provides other agency officials who are not on the board advance notice regarding the details of IG planned actions, which could impair sensitive or confidential work by the IG. Participants noted that there are provisions that allow a Data Integrity Board decision to be appealed to the Office of Management and Budget; however, they did not believe this was a remedy to the independence impairment.

- *The IG community has sought a legislative exemption from the Computer Matching Act.* IG community participants stated that they believed oversight and law enforcement entities should be exempt from Computer Matching Act requirements. Although recognizing the importance of Privacy Act protections, IG community participants commented that they believed the ability to perform data matching to identify fraud, waste, and abuse outweighs the privacy protection provided by the act. CIGIE has publicly supported a legislative exemption to allow IG offices greater ability to match data for oversight and law enforcement purposes. Several government participants noted the need to update existing requirements that were developed several decades ago to account for technology changes and current privacy concerns. Private-sector participants agreed that legislation has lagged behind technology, affecting how experts can utilize available data.

Data Standards Vary across the Government, Limiting the Ease of Sharing Data

Participants said that federal and state government agencies are not working from a single set of data standards, which limits the ability of the participant's agency to share and use data because of difficulty in integrating systems and interpreting varying definitions for data elements.

---

[6]Each federal agency must establish an internal Data Integrity Board to oversee and coordinate its data matching activities.

One participant said that the lack of uniformity hinders her agency's ability to quickly put data to use. Another said that the lack of standards leads to difficulties for the oversight community.

One participant highlighted a lack of standards and interoperability of state systems designed to administer federal programs as a particular challenge in conducting oversight. This participant explained that federal agencies require states to set up their own data systems to manage federally funded programs without offering a data standard guideline. Another participant cited Medicaid as an example of a federally supported program that could better define data requirements. Because of this, when federal oversight offices subsequently attempt to audit federally funded programs administered by states, federal auditors sometimes have difficulty interpreting the data because the states collect data based on their own individual data standards. One participant with experience working for a state agency said that the federal government could establish national criteria that the states could incorporate when developing systems, and that such systems could be reviewed by the funding agency to ensure consistency prior to implementation of the data system. Such an approach could ensure the development of a set of national data standards and would allow for the seamless sharing of information by all participating entities, according to the participant. Several participants believed the federal government is in the best position to set these standards since the impetus of these programs begins with the granting of federal funding.

Participants provided examples of uniform standards that could assist in improving interoperability of data and systems, which could better enable federal, state, and local governments to collaborate to share and use data. For example:

- Some participants said that a universal identification naming-convention standard for awards, or "universal award ID," is one such uniform standard that could improve interoperability and help cross-agency efforts.[7] A unique government-wide universal award ID for all federal contracts, grants, and loans would make it much easier to track and reconcile funds awarded to recipients of federal funds,

---

[7]An award ID is the number that agencies assign to contracts, grants, and loans. There is currently no requirement that award IDs be standardized across the government.

according to one participant.

- One participant said that to make data sharing useful, "identity resolution" should be a key consideration in developing datasets. Identity resolution involves using common identifiers—such as Social Security Numbers or Employer Identification Numbers—across datasets to allow agencies to accurately identify individuals and entities, which is critical to matching records in datasets.

- Another participant said that a data dictionary ensures everyone is using the same definitions.

Lack of Incentives and Independence Issues Hinder Sharing between Program Offices and the Oversight Community

Participants said that program offices often lack incentives to share data they collect with the oversight community. For example, some forum participants said that agency program offices—which often are the collectors and owners of data—can feel threatened by oversight agencies. Multiple participants attributed reluctance in sharing to a lack of trust between program and oversight entities. One participant added that agencies invest a lot of resources into developing data and may feel their data are proprietary and, as a consequence, may not want to give it away for free. Participants offered ideas on better incentivizing program offices to share their data. For example, while asking program offices to become more auditable may not be a convincing argument, one participant noted that oversight entities could better seize opportunities to build bridges between program and oversight entities by treating program offices like useful resources and allies. Forum participants agreed that fostering a more collaborative relationship could incentivize program offices to build systems and provide data that are more useful for oversight operations.

Further, participants from the IG community raised questions about the extent to which they can share data analytics tools and the results of using those tools with agencies that would help agencies prevent fraud, waste, and abuse and yet still maintain independence. For example, one participant noted that the IG office shares certain information on effective ways to identify fraud with the agency it oversees in order for the agency to develop a process for preventing future similar fraudulent activities rather than trying to recover the payment after it has been made. The participant said that his office would like to share its analytics tools and the results therefrom; however, sharing such tools and information can create concerns about independence. For example, an IG's sharing of such tools and information with the agency it oversees could raise questions about the IG's independence under *Government Auditing*

Standards if the IG is perceived as directing the agency to implement specific management practices and then later audits these practices.[8]

State and Local Participants Experienced a Number of Challenges to Sharing Data and Knowledge across Levels of Government

Participants stated that collaboration and cooperation between and among federal, state, and local stakeholders could help all levels of government prevent and detect fraud, waste, and abuse; but a number of challenges exist to sharing data and information between entities.

- *State and local participants highlighted actual and perceived legislative barriers that limit federal sharing across levels of government.* One participant with experience working for a local government recalled a recent instance when city auditors who were performing an audit related to the city's evaluation of client services for its human immunodeficiency virus (HIV) services program encountered legal barriers. Specifically, city auditors were evaluating whether HIV services jointly paid for by the city, state, and federal government were actually being received by clients in need. The auditors requested client-verification data from federal and state agencies to assist them in their efforts; however, the agencies objected to providing data, citing concerns about the Health Insurance Portability and Accountability Act (HIPAA)—which was enacted in part to safeguard protected health information from unauthorized use and disclosure. Additionally, participants said that some oversight and law enforcement entities at state and local levels perceive barriers that may not actually exist. For example, some participants with experience working for state or local governments said that state and local entities do not have legal authority to access databases containing certain federal data, such as identity verification through the Social Security Administration, federal Do Not Pay lists, and prisoner data and incarceration records. However, one federal participant countered that state and local entities may believe they do not have such legal authority, when in actuality there may be no federal laws preventing state and local agencies from accessing some of the databases mentioned. For example, this participant said there is nothing in the law that prohibits state and local entities from accessing federal Do Not Pay lists. Such issues—whether they are an accurate interpretation of existing law or potentially incorrect perceptions—may hinder efforts to stop improper payments at the

---

[8]Steps to address this issue and other challenges identified at the forum are covered in the final section of this report.

state and local levels, according to participants.

- *Some data are cost-prohibitive to obtain.* One participant commented that the cost of commercial data is an impediment to developing and using analytics capabilities in the government. This participant explained that private-sector companies and some governmental agencies impose fees for access to their data. One example participants cited is the Social Security Administration's Death Master File (DMF).[9] The DMF can be used to ensure government benefits are not being provided to deceased individuals; however, an agency wishing to use the DMF must pay fees that some participants said were too costly for their agencies.[10] One forum participant said that his office received a quote of over $50,000 for a 1-year subscription to the DMF with monthly updates.

- *Limited coordination between federal, state, and local oversight entities sometimes causes missed opportunities and redundancy in auditing activities.* State and local participants reported that information is not readily shared even when state or local governments are working toward the same goals as the federal government on related or identical efforts. For example, a participant with experience working for a local government described a situation in which the participant's city was performing an audit of a municipal wastewater-treatment facility. The participant said that nearly identical audits were being performed simultaneously by federal and state auditors. Although auditors from each level of government were aware of the other concurrent audits, there was little effort to determine whether they could work together in an effort to avoid duplicative work and conserve scarce resources. This official also noted that there are instances in which a federal agency will conduct and complete an audit or investigation of a city office, with the city only to be informally notified after the audit or investigation has been done, which creates the potential for redundant audits. Additionally, a forum participant with experience working for a state oversight entity said that there is no mechanism within the federal government to identify and leverage

---

[9]The DMF is maintained by the Social Security Administration and contains approximately 98 million records of deaths that have been reported since 1936. The file is used by government; credit-reporting organizations; and financial, investigative, medical research, and other industries to verify deaths.

[10]The Social Security Administration has statutory authority to require reimbursement to cover the reasonable cost of sharing the data, and the amount varies by agency.

the results of state-government audits in related federal investigations. Such a mechanism to share information would allow the federal government to incorporate relevant knowledge garnered at the state level, according to the participant.

- *State and local government offices are sometimes reluctant to share data with the federal government.* A forum participant with experience in local government oversight said that local governments may be reluctant to share more than the required amount of data with state and federal agencies because data sharing seemed to be a "one-way street," with local offices providing referrals to federal and state entities but getting nothing in return.

Opportunities Exist to Develop, Enhance, and Leverage Open-Source Data-Analytics Modules and Tools to Facilitate Knowledge Sharing

During the forum, participants stated that there is a need to share analytical processes and algorithms to better benefit oversight and law enforcement communities. The discussion in particular concentrated on the benefits of utilizing interoperable, open-source analytical tools and techniques, including open-source software. One participant encouraged the use of open-source tools because they can be utilized at a low cost, can be adjusted to meet the needs of individual agencies relatively easily, and have large support communities that agencies can tap for guidance. Two participants also noted that the use of open-source tools could lessen the challenge of developing licensing agreements for proprietary software tools. Some participants suggested that open-source tools and algorithms could be consolidated in a central location to allow for ease of access across these communities to better identify fraud, waste, and abuse.

Forum Participants Identified Next Steps in Addressing Challenges

Throughout the day, forum participants identified a variety of challenges that hinder their abilities to share and use data, as well as several areas where opportunities may exist to improve their abilities to use data to identify fraud, waste, and abuse. During the final session of the forum, participants shared their views on how federal oversight and law enforcement agencies might address these challenges and capitalize on opportunities. Participants discussed ways federal agencies could raise awareness of available data, improve access to information, and identify statutory changes that may be necessary to overcome challenges associated with sharing and matching data. Specifically, participants suggested the following next steps:

- *Compile a consolidated directory of data sources.* One theme that emerged during the forum is that oversight and law enforcement entities are often not aware of the data at other federal agencies or publicly available data that could aid their missions. Participants discussed the benefits of a detailed directory of existing data sources used to identify fraud, waste, and abuse that could be referred to by oversight and law enforcement entities. CIGIE and the Recovery Board agreed to colead an effort to provide a means to increase awareness of useful datasets.

- *Compile a dataset of known offenders.* During the forum, participants discussed the need for greater sharing of information, particularly on known offenders. Oversight and law enforcement entities have case-management systems, but participants cited reluctance to share data on known offenders. Participants believed that centralizing information on such individuals—while bearing in mind any potential privacy-protection concerns—would yield benefits in the detection and prevention of fraud. CIGIE and the Recovery Board agreed to colead an effort to increase awareness of known offenders.

- *Address statutory challenges related to data access and use.* Participants discussed the importance of examining the existing statutory framework to determine whether statutory changes would be useful to oversight and law enforcement agencies in carrying out their missions. CIGIE reported that it has an existing committee to analyze legislation and, as deemed necessary by its participants, develop legislative proposals recommending changes to existing and proposed statutory provisions. CIGIE offered to make this existing committee available as a vehicle to expand a discussion of current law, and, as appropriate, to continue to identify changes to existing and proposed statutory provisions that create challenges and barriers affecting audit and law enforcement data access and use.

- *Address questions about the Government Auditing Standards independence requirement.* The IG community raised questions about the extent to which they can share results with agencies that would help agencies prevent fraud, waste, and abuse, and yet still maintain independence necessary for conducting effective oversight. Participants saw value in having GAO—which develops and issues the *Government Auditing Standards*—provide clarification regarding the independence standard. As a result, GAO agreed to provide clarification related to the independence standard of the *Government Auditing Standards*.

- *Develop an ongoing community of practice focused on data-sharing challenges.* Throughout the forum, participants cited the need for greater coordination and incentives to share information among federal, state, and local government agencies as well as among federal government agencies. For example, one participant said that there is no mechanism within the federal government to identify and leverage the results of state-government audits in related federal investigations. Another participant said that agencies that invest a lot of resources into developing data may have cultural resistance to giving it away for free. To address these and other issues related to coordination and data sharing, GAO will be forming a community of practice that will address issues related to data and information sharing across federal, state, and local governments, as well as sharing data among federal agencies.

- *Compile a library of available open-source data analytics, modules, and tools.* Forum participants said that sharing algorithms and analytics tools would help to improve efficiencies and suggested that consolidating open-source software, algorithms, and data-analytics tools could help oversight entities in their audits, inspections, evaluations, and investigations. CIGIE and the Recovery Board will be working together to compile and maintain this library.

Appendix I: Forum Agenda

Data Analytics for Oversight and Law Enforcement
January 16, 2013
8:30 a.m. to 3:40 p.m.

8:30 a.m.	**Registration** Continental breakfast	McCarl Room, 7C21
9:00 a.m. to 9:25 a.m.	**Opening Speakers** Gene L. Dodaro, Comptroller General of the U.S. Phyllis K. Fong, Chairperson, CIGIE Kathleen S. Tighe, Chair, Recovery Board	Staats Briefing Room, 7C13
9:25 a.m. to 10:10 a.m.	**Data Sources**	Staats Briefing Room, 7C13 Facilitator: Erika Axelson Assistant Director, GAO
10:10 a.m. to 10:25 a.m.	**Break**	
10:25 a.m. to 11:40 a.m.	**Access to and Sharing of Data**	Staats Briefing Room, 7C13 Facilitator: Carrie Hug Director, Accountability, Recovery Board
11:40 a.m. to 1:10 p.m.	**Working Lunch** **Technology Tools**	McCarl Room, 7C21 (lunch pickup) Staats Briefing Room, 7C13 Facilitator: Shawn Kingsberry Chief Information Officer, Recovery Board
1:10 p.m. to 2:25 p.m.	**Managing and Using Data**	Staats Briefing Room, 7C13 Facilitator: Gary Cantrell Deputy Inspector General for Investigations, HHS-OIG
2:25 p.m. to 2:40 p.m.	**Break**	
2:40 p.m. to 3:40 p.m.	**Next Steps**	Staats Briefing Room, 7C13 Facilitators: Gene L. Dodaro, Comptroller General Phyllis K. Fong, Chairperson, CIGIE Kathleen S. Tighe, Chair, Recovery Board

Appendix II: Forum Participants

Data Analytics for Oversight and Law Enforcement

Participant List

Name	Title, Organization
Co-hosts	
Gene L. Dodaro	Comptroller General of the United States, U.S. Government Accountability Office
Phyllis K. Fong	Chairperson Council of the Inspectors General on Integrity and Efficiency; Inspector General U.S. Department of Agriculture
Kathleen S. Tighe	Chair Recovery Accountability and Transparency Board; Inspector General U.S. Department of Education
Facilitators	
Erika Axelson	Assistant Director Forensic Audits and Investigative Service U.S. Government Accountability Office
Carrie Hug	Director of Accountability Recovery Accountability and Transparency Board
Shawn Kingsberry	Assistant Director of Technology and Chief Information Officer Recovery Accountability and Transparency Board
Gary Cantrell	Deputy Inspector General for Investigations Office of Inspector General U.S. Department of Health and Human Services
Participants	
Rex Ahlstrom	Chief Strategy Officer BackOffice Associates

Brett M. Baker Assistant Inspector General for Audit
Office of Inspector General
National Science Foundation

Jason R. Baron Director of Litigation
National Archives and Records Administration

Cathleen Berrick Managing Director
Forensic Audits and Investigative Service
Homeland Security and Justice
U.S. Government Accountability Office

Stu Bradley Director
Fraud and Financial Crimes Practice
SAS

Charles Coe Assistant Inspector General
Office of Inspector General
U.S. Department of Education

Donald I. Cox Deputy Director of Accountability
Recovery Accountability and Transparency Board

Patricia Dalton Chief Operating Officer
U.S. Government Accountability Office

Rod DeSmet Deputy Assistant Inspector General for Audit
Office of Inspector General
U.S. Department of Agriculture

James Duginske Deputy Assistant Director
Recovery Operations Center
Recovery Accountability and Transparency Board

Kelly Gent Director
Data Analytics and Control Group
Centers for Medicare & Medicaid Services

Glenn Harris Counsel to the Inspector General
Office of Inspector General
U.S. Small Business Administration

Gregory A. Hook Deputy Legislative Auditor
Maryland Office of Legislative Audits

Bryan Jones Director of Data Mining Group
Office of Inspector General
U.S. Postal Service

Larry Koskinen	Assistant Inspector General for Strategy and Analytics
	Office of Inspector General
	U.S. Postal Service
Andy Mao	Assistant Director
	Civil Division, Commercial Litigation Branch
	U.S. Department of Justice
Gerhard Pilcher	Vice President and Senior Scientist
	Elder Research, Inc.
David Plocher	Deputy Assistant General Counsel
	U.S. Government Accountability Office
Dominic Sale	Supervisory Policy Analyst
	Office of Management and Budget
Steven Shandy	Supervisory Program Manager
	Consolidated Data Analysis Center
	Office of Inspector General
	U.S. Department of Health and Human Services
Edward Slevin	Director of Computer Aided Audit Tools
	Office of Inspector General
	U.S. Department of Education
Allison Stanton	Director of E-Discovery
	Civil Division
	U.S. Department of Justice
Corrie Stokes	Deputy City Auditor
	City of Austin, Texas
Chris Swecker	Chief Executive Officer
	Chris Swecker Enterprises
Pamela Vanderburg	Acting Section Chief
	Financial Crimes Section
	Federal Bureau of Investigation
Kawai Washburn	Forward Deployed Engineer
	Palantir Technologies
Michael Wood	Executive Director
	Recovery Accountability and Transparency Board

Appendix III: Related Products and Image Sources

GAO	*Social Security Administration: Preliminary Observations on the Death Master File.* GAO-13-574T. Washington, D.C.: May 8, 2013.
	Human Services: Sustained and Coordinated Efforts Could Facilitate Data Sharing While Protecting Privacy. GAO-13-106. Washington, D.C.: February 8, 2013.
	Medicare Fraud Prevention: CMS Has Implemented a Predictive Analytics System, but Needs to Define Measures to Determine Its Effectiveness. GAO-13-104. Washington, D.C.: October 15, 2012.
	Privacy: Federal Law Should Be Updated to Address Changing Technology Landscape. GAO-12-961T. Washington, D.C.: July 31, 2012.
	Federal Statistical System: Agencies Can Make Greater Use of Existing Data, but Continued Progress Is Needed on Access and Quality Issues. GAO-12-54. Washington, D.C.: February 24, 2012.
	Improper Payments: Moving Forward with Governmentwide Reduction Strategies. GAO-12-405T. Washington, D.C.: February 7, 2012.
	TANF and Child Welfare Programs: Increased Data Sharing Could Improve Access to Benefits and Services. GAO-12-2. Washington, D.C.: October 7, 2011.
	Privacy: Alternatives Exist for Enhancing Protection of Personally Identifiable Information. GAO-08-536. Washington, D.C.: May 19, 2008.
	*Data Mining: Federal Efforts Cover a Wide Range of Use*s. GAO-04-548. Washington, D.C.: May 4, 2004.
Council of the Inspectors General on Integrity and Efficiency	Phyllis K. Fong, Inspector General, U.S. Department of Agriculture. *American Recovery and Reinvestment Act—Review of the Effectiveness of Department/Agency Data Quality Review Processes.* Memorandum to the Recovery Accountability and Transparency Board. Washington, D.C.: June 25, 2010. http://www.usda.gov/oig/webdocs/50703-2-DA.pdf
	Office of Inspector General, U.S. Department of Agriculture. American Recovery and *Reinvestment Act—Review of the Effectiveness of Department/Agency Data Quality Review Processes.* Audit Report 50703-1-DA. Washington, D.C.: June 2010. http://www.usda.gov/oig/webdocs/50703-1-DA.pdf

Office of Inspector General, U.S. Department of Education. *Recovery Act Data Quality: Recipient Efforts to Report Reliable and Transparent Information.* Memorandum to the Recovery Accountability and Transparency Board. Washington, D.C.: September 13, 2010. http://www2.ed.gov/about/offices/list/oig/auditreports/fy2010/s20k0002.pdf

Office of Inspector General, U.S. Department of Agriculture. *Analysis of FNS' Supplemental Nutrition Assistance Program Fraud Prevention and Detection Efforts.* Audit Report 27002-0011-13. Washington, D.C.: September 2012. http://www.usda.gov/oig/webdocs/27002-0011-13.pdf

Recovery Accountability and Transparency Board	Office of Inspector General, U.S. Department of Education. *American Recovery and Reinvestment Act: The Effectiveness of the Department's Data Quality Review Processes.* Final Audit Report, ED-OIG/A19K0010. August 2011. http://www.recovery.gov/Accountability/inspectors/Documents/a19k0010-Effectiveness%20of%20Dept's%20Data%20Quality%20Review%20Processes.pdf

Office of Inspector General, U.S. Department of Transportation. *Recovery Act Data Quality: Errors in Recipients' Reports Obscure Transparency.* Washington, D.C.: February 23, 2010. http://www.recovery.gov/Accountability/inspectors/Documents/Data%20Quality%20Phase%20II%20Final%20Report.pdf

Office of the Inspector General, U.S. Department of Justice. *Review of Department of Justice Data Quality Procedures for Recovery Act Recipient Reports.* Washington, D.C.: October 2009. http://www.recovery.gov/Accountability/inspectors/Documents/DOJ%20Data%20Quality%20Review%20Report%2010-30-09%20Final.pdf

Solutions for Accountability and Transparency: Uniform Governmentwide Award ID Number. n.d. http://www.recovery.gov/About/Documents/WhitePaperonStandardizedGovernmentwideAwardID.pdf

National Academy of Public Administration. A Recovery Dialogue on IT Solutions: After-Action Report. A report prepared for The Hon. Earl E. Devaney, Chairman, Recovery Accountability and Transparency Board, and G. Edward DeSeve, Special Advisor to the President, Recovery Implementation. Washington, D.C.: May 2009.

http://www.recovery.gov/About/Documents/NAPA_Recovery_Dialogue_Fi
nal_Report_5-20-09_0.pdf

Image Sources

This section contains credit and copyright information for images and
graphics in this report.

Front cover: PhotoDisc (globe), GAO (GAO logo), Council of the
Inspectors General on Integrity and Efficiency (CIGIE logo), Recovery
Accountability and Transparency Board (Recovery Board seal)

Highlights page: PhotoDisc (globe), GAO (GAO logo), Council of the
Inspectors General on Integrity and Efficiency (CIGIE logo), Recovery
Accountability and Transparency Board (Recovery Board seal)

Appendix IV: Contacts and Staff Acknowledgments

Contacts

GAO	Steve M. Lord, (202) 512-4379 or lords@gao.gov
Council of the Inspectors General on Integrity and Efficiency	Mark Jones, (202) 292-2600 or CIGIE.Information@cigie.gov
Recovery Accountability and Transparency Board	Michael Wood, (202) 254-7900 or michael.wood@ratb.gov

Staff Acknowledgments

GAO	In addition to the contact named above, Patricia Dalton, Chief Operating Officer; Nabajyoti Barkakati, Chief Technologist; Cathleen A. Berrick, Managing Director; Rick Hillman, Managing Director; Erika Axelson, Assistant Director; Jennifer Costello, Assistant Director; Joah Iannotta, Assistant Director; Jamie L. Berryhill; Marcus Corbin; Ranya Elias; Robert Graves; Linda Miller; and Maria McMullen made important contributions to organizing the forum and producing this report.
Council of the Inspectors General on Integrity and Efficiency	In addition to the contact named above, Gary Cantrell and Steve Shandy, U.S. Department of Health and Human Services Office of Inspector General; Charles Coe, U.S. Department of Education Office of Inspector General; and Rod DeSmet; U.S. Department of Agriculture Office of Inspector General, made important contributions to organizing the forum and producing this report.
Recovery Accountability and Transparency Board	In addition to the contact named above, Jenny Rone, Senior Advisor for Accountability, made important contributions to organizing the forum and producing this report.

GAO's Mission	The Government Accountability Office, the audit, evaluation, and investigative arm of Congress, exists to support Congress in meeting its constitutional responsibilities and to help improve the performance and accountability of the federal government for the American people. GAO examines the use of public funds; evaluates federal programs and policies; and provides analyses, recommendations, and other assistance to help Congress make informed oversight, policy, and funding decisions. GAO's commitment to good government is reflected in its core values of accountability, integrity, and reliability.
Obtaining Copies of GAO Reports and Testimony	The fastest and easiest way to obtain copies of GAO documents at no cost is through GAO's website (http://www.gao.gov). Each weekday afternoon, GAO posts on its website newly released reports, testimony, and correspondence. To have GAO e-mail you a list of newly posted products, go to http://www.gao.gov and select "E-mail Updates."
Order by Phone	The price of each GAO publication reflects GAO's actual cost of production and distribution and depends on the number of pages in the publication and whether the publication is printed in color or black and white. Pricing and ordering information is posted on GAO's website, http://www.gao.gov/ordering.htm. Place orders by calling (202) 512-6000, toll free (866) 801-7077, or TDD (202) 512-2537. Orders may be paid for using American Express, Discover Card, MasterCard, Visa, check, or money order. Call for additional information.
Connect with GAO	Connect with GAO on Facebook, Flickr, Twitter, and YouTube. Subscribe to our RSS Feeds or E-mail Updates. Listen to our Podcasts. Visit GAO on the web at www.gao.gov.
To Report Fraud, Waste, and Abuse in Federal Programs	Contact: Website: http://www.gao.gov/fraudnet/fraudnet.htm E-mail: fraudnet@gao.gov Automated answering system: (800) 424-5454 or (202) 512-7470
Congressional Relations	Katherine Siggerud, Managing Director, siggerudk@gao.gov, (202) 512-4400, U.S. Government Accountability Office, 441 G Street NW, Room 7125, Washington, DC 20548
Public Affairs	Chuck Young, Managing Director, youngc1@gao.gov, (202) 512-4800 U.S. Government Accountability Office, 441 G Street NW, Room 7149 Washington, DC 20548